Original title:
Acanthus Anecdotes

Copyright © 2025 Creative Arts Management OÜ
All rights reserved.

Author: Tobias Sterling
ISBN HARDBACK: 978-1-80567-025-4
ISBN PAPERBACK: 978-1-80567-105-3

Reflections Among the Stems

In gardens bright, they often prance,
With leaves like hats, they twirl and dance.
The blooms do giggle, the thorns just sigh,
As bees play cards, and butterflies fly.

A snail put on a hat one day,
Said, 'This slow life is the only way!'
While worms debate on the best warm stew,
'They should try s'mores, now that's something new!'

The Palette of the Flowering Earth

Colors clash in a vibrant spree,
Roses wear pants, just wait and see!
Daisies chuckle at lilies dressed fine,
'Who needs a suit? We'll all be divine!'

A daffodil whispered, 'I'm feeling bold!'
While violets claimed they were far too old.
Yet when the sun began to creep,
All did agree—time for a nap, not a peep!

Humble Narrations from the Thicket

In brambles wild, tales twist and turn,
The ladybug told of her great concern.
'What if I flit, and the wind just scoffs?
Or the next surprise is a frog that coughs?'

The squirrels chuckle with acorns aplenty,
While rabbits partake in the drama, quite gentry.
'Let's host a show!' one carrot exclaimed,
'With all that we see, we'll surely be famed!'

The Language of Lost Petals

Once petals fell in a gossip spree,
'The rose over there thinks she's so free!'
Chrysanthemums giggled, 'Her scent's a delight,
But her gossip's sharper than a thorny bite!'

With whispers of blooms on the soft summer air,
Each petal replaced, but none had a care.
'Tell a joke!' wished the daisies in chorus,
While the tulips just danced, saying, 'What's the fuss for?'

The Graceful Undergrowth

In a garden lush and sly,
The plants began to giggle and sigh.
A flower tripped on leafy shoes,
And whispered tales of silly blues.

The bushes swayed with laughter bright,
As a worm wiggled left, then right.
They planned a party on a whim,
To dance beneath the tree's great brim.

Impressions of Verdant Dreams

Once in a forest green and wide,
The ferns took bets on who would ride.
A squirrel hopped on a mushroom fair,
Claiming it was his private lair.

The sunbeams played a shining tune,
While bees buzzed round like tiny balloons.
A rabbit joined with a flip and twist,
Declaring, 'This party can't be missed!'

Vine-Spun Chronicles

Vines wrapped round a sleeping tree,
Said, 'Wake up, it's time for tea!'
They brewed a cup from morning dew,
And invited all the critters too.

A hedgehog brought his prickly flair,
While a snail slid in, real slow and rare.
They toasted to the brightest moon,
And shared a laugh with every tune.

Echoes Among the Petals

Pansies whispered secrets bold,
About a bee who'd turned to gold.
He sang a tune, it made them sway,
And all the petals danced away.

The daisies chuckled, 'What a sight!'
While butterflies took off in flight.
A wise old tulip joined the fun,
Saying, 'Let's play till day is done!'

Lullabies of the Leafy Canopy

In a garden where leaves giggle and sway,
A snail once raced a leaf in dismay.
The leaf just laughed and rolled right on by,
While the snail grumbled, 'Why don't I fly?'

A beetle wore shades and danced to a tune,
While crickets chirped madly beneath the full moon.
They waved to the flowers, all dressed in their best,
'Come join our party, leave worries to rest!'

A squirrel in stripes tried to join in the fun,
But tripped on his tail and fell with a thud,
The flowers all chuckled, a cacophony bright,
'Look at our friend, what a comical sight!'

As night drew near, the leaves hummed a song,
Of adventures and mishaps that never felt wrong.
In the funny old woods, the laughter won't cease,
For every small creature finds joy and finds peace.

Curved Fables of the Earth

In gardens where insects wear shoes,
There's gossip afloat; they spread funny news.
The daisies wear hats, quite cleverly done,
While roses debate who's the prettiest one.

The clover's in shorts, feeling quite bold,
While the daisies sell lemonade, icy and cold.
A grasshopper jumps, but he trips on a bee,
And the whole flower crowd starts laughing with glee.

They tell tales of worms that do tango at night,
While snails take a stroll under pale moonlight.
The beetles are tucked in a bed made of leaves,
They snore as the night breeze gives soft, funny heaves.

So next time you stroll through that magical space,
Look closely and see all the jokes that you face.
The earth tells a story, all twisted and curled,
With laughter and cheer, it brightens the world.

The Rooted Storyteller

A tree with a grin, quite full of delight,
Stands whispering tales till the sun goes to night.
With roots like arms, it beckons us near,
To spill all its secrets, full of good cheer.

From squirrels that barter acorns for tales,
To shadows that dance in soft, breezy trails,
The knots in its bark are a map of old jest,
Each ring tells a story, a humor-filled quest.

The parsnips at times pull practical pranks,
Making veggies laugh, or are they just yanks?
"Don't take us for granted," the peas start to shout,
"We've got mighty humor, let's twist this thing out!"

So listen intently, join in the fun,
With laughter and stories, there's plenty for one.
In the heart of the garden, where roots intertwine,
The stories are plenty, both silly and fine.

Blooms Beneath the Surface

Under the soil, where it's cozy and dark,
The flowers have meetings; they're making a spark.
The tulips wear glasses and gather around,
To debate their fine colors; they laugh with a sound.

The daisies chip in with their own funny quips,
While the shy little violets share awkward slips.
The ants bring the snacks; they're the life of the show,
Though last week on a trip, they forgot where to go!

Hydrangeas gossip about bees and their flight,
While the peonies chuckle at spiders' next fright.
They've seen all the blunders of creatures above,
With humor that feels like a warm, fuzzy glove.

So dig down below, and you'll surely find,
A world bubbling over with laughter entwined.
Each blossom a story, each leaf holds a laugh,
In the garden's grand play, they're the fun-loving staff.

Where the Wild Twists

In a field where the mischief of nature abounds,
The flowers are funny, they throw jolly bounds.
The sunflowers gossip while twisting their heads,
Saying, "Watch out! There's another bad pun ahead!"

The daisies perform their comedic charades,
While the wind joins the act with comedic cascades.
The poppies wear capes while taking a bow,
As the ferns roll their eyes at the antics, somehow.

A butterfly flits, but then trips on a twig,
Causing the blooms to burst forth and gig.
"Watch where you're landing!" the roses all scream,
"It's not just a fumble; it's plant warfare theme!"

So if you should wander to where wildness reigns,
Embrace every twist, let go of the chains.
For laughter is blooming in every odd place,
In fields of pure mirth, find the joy in the space.

Shadows of the Ornate Fronds

In the garden's shadiest nook,
A squirrel writes a rhyming book.
With fronds that twist and curl so wide,
He thinks his poetry's bona fide.

The daisies dance with glee, they swear,
His verses give them quite a scare.
With each strange line, they giggle, tease,
'It's a bushy bard's bizarre disease!'

The hedgehog rolls his eyes and sighs,
As ferns gossip with leafy lies.
They claim the poet's lost his mind,
A frond with humor, hard to find.

But under shadows, secrets bloom,
A vulture hums a gentle tune.
The ornate fronds reveal the jest,
In every leaf, laughter's the best.

Echoes in the Verdant Shadows

Amidst the leaves, a laughter echoes,
A lizard dons a hat like Pippin's.
He struts around, a fancy sight,
With tiny shoes, his pride takes flight.

The crickets chirp a cheeky song,
As if to say, 'Ain't this long?
The shadows dance, they twist and sway,
In leafy halls where whispers play.'

When daylight fades, the punchlines bloom,
In every crevice, jokes find room.
It's a funny world of green delights,
Where shadows tell of mischief nights.

The wise old owl, with winking eye,
Declares that laughter will not die.
He chuckles deep in verdant clime,
'A jest shared is laughter most sublime!'

Legends of the Regal Foliage

In a land where foliage holds court,
A queen of leaves invites to sport.
The branches sway, their secrets swell,
In a leafy tale, all's quite well.

The playful winds whisper witty jibes,
As daisies tease the thistles' tribes.
A royal shade from roots to tips,
With riddles that can twist the lips.

The bees wear crowns of golden glaze,
In this kingdom of leafy plays.
They tell of knights with thorny swords,
In battles fought with frond rewards.

The sun slips low, and soon the night,
Brings tales of laughter, pure delight.
Regal foliage, bright and bold,
In every leaf, new legends told.

The Enigma of the Leafy Spiral

In spirals deep, a secret spins,
A snail in shades of emerald grins.
He claims to know the ancient lore,
Of leafy paths and endless stores.

The tussocks laugh when he regales,
Of whispered winds and leafy tales.
With each turn, a chuckle's freed,
A comical twist in every deed.

The ladybugs hold court with grace,
As laughter turns the garden space.
They tumble down from high above,
In spirals of giggles and leafy love.

So when you see a spiral twine,
Remember the fun that grows in rhyme.
For in each leaf, a smile's unfurled,
And mystery wraps this leafy world.

The Language of Thorns

In a garden rife with prickle,
Petals played their secret trickle.
Whispered tales of woe and glee,
Beware the blooms, they'll poke thee!

Gossipy vines tangled in rhymes,
Joking, laughing, passing times.
Thorns poke fun at all they see,
'Tis the price of a flowery spree!

A blunt rose murmured to a daisy,
'Your polka dots are looking hazy.'
While the sunflowers grinned so wide,
As the lilies took their leafy ride.

In the flowery hub, it's quite absurd,
Every petal's gossip can be heard.
A cactus joins the lively jest,
"With you here, I feel quite blessed!"

Secrets in the Silhouette

In twilight's glow, the shadows dance,
Every leaf in a sly romance.
The petals whisper tales at night,
Floral secrets, quite the sight!

A dandelion, proud and bold,
Claims its wisdom never told.
"Float away! Don't plant your roots,
Life's a joke in wilted suits!"

On soft moss, the mushrooms creep,
Holding secrets they can't keep.
Fungi giggle, making plans,
While the ferns mimic the fans.

In moonlit gardens, laughter swells,
Every plant has funny tales to tell.
With shadows casting comic rays,
Nature's jesters earn their praise!

Flora's Embrace

In a meadow, blooms convene,
Petal pickles, quite the scene!
Sunlight grins upon their heads,
Spilling jokes on flower beds.

The violets blush at palm fronds,
While daffodils plot their response.
"Let's prank the busy honeybee,
And make it think we're all a tree!"

A pansy winks with floral flair,
"Did you hear? The roses dare!
To wear a crown of buttercups,
For planting seeds in clever ups!"

In spring's embrace, they giggle loud,
Nature's jesters in a crowd.
With playful whispers in the breeze,
They tickle all with leafy tease!

Tales from the Garden Path

Strolling down the garden track,
Flowers giggle, wave not lack.
"Here comes trouble!" blooms declare,
Holding tales with fragrant air!

A pansy painted with a pout,
Boasts about the bees' mishap route.
"Buzz off, you bloomless doofus!"
Blossoms share each silly ruckus.

The peonies discuss their shades,
And how sunburn's the latest craze.
"Don't fret," says one with vivid hue,
"We'll just wear hats made of dew!"

Among the weeds, a party brews,
With roots and stems in colorful shoes.
Every petal sways and spins,
Reveling in the joy they bring!

Labyrinth of the Leafy Heart

In the garden, there's a maze,
Where plants play silly games for days.
A pumpkin wears a funny hat,
And sings to every passing cat.

The daisies whisper wild tales,
Of sneaky snails and fuzzy quails.
The trees chuckle, sharing jokes,
While rabbits act like silly folks.

Down by the brook, frogs leap with glee,
Dancing to tunes of a bumblebee.
Each petal holds a giggling round,
In the leafy labyrinth profound.

Sunlight filters, laughter spreads,
As nature spins its tale in threads.
Every leaf and twig does its part,
In the madness of a leafy heart.

Nature's Endless Chronicle

Once a squirrel stole a shoe,
To impress a bird he once knew.
They giggled by the old oak tree,
Claiming it was 'fashion history.'

Butterflies, with their wily ways,
Tell secrets of the dandiest days.
While crickets play their tiny tunes,
Under the watch of grinning moons.

The flowers gossip, full of cheer,
About the frolics that they hear.
Every breeze is filled with laughter,
In nature's tales and joyful afters.

And so the forest pens its lore,
Of funny creatures forevermore.
In every leaf, a smile's sparked,
Nature's endless chronicle, well-marked.

Lingering in the Leafy Realm

In a thicket where shadows play,
A rabbit tells tall tales all day.
With floppy ears, he holds the crowd,
While dancing 'neath a sky so proud.

The ferns sway with a latest trend,
As ivy takes a twirl and bends.
Each patch of moss has something to share,
Of silly moments filled with flair.

A hedgehog dons a tiny coat,
Practicing his stand-up note.
He wobbles 'round with comic flair,
As laughter lingers in the air.

So in this leafy, vibrant land,
Everyone finds joy, hand in hand.
In giggles, stories bloom and scream,
Lingering in nature's leafy dream.

Stories Woven in Green

A caterpillar stretched and sighed,
'What's with this munching bug beside?'
They swapped their tales of tedious fate,
And hatched a plan to celebrate.

Beneath the blooms where shadows sway,
Bees buzz about their grand ballet.
With petals soft and colors bright,
They dance from morn till fall of night.

The willow weeps but makes it fun,
With droopy arms that play and run.
Each drip from leaves, a giggly stare,
In this green realm where jokes are rare.

So gather 'round, the stories flow,
Of nature's quirks and woodland show.
In every nook, a laugh unseen,
In the stories woven in green.

When Leaves Speak

The leaves gossip softly, oh what a tale,
Of the squirrel who slipped, and began to flail.
They chuckle and rustle, quite merry indeed,
As the breeze joins the laughter, fulfilling their need.

A ladybug danced, with spots all aglow,
But tripped on a twig, causing quite the show.
The branches all giggled, in branches they sway,
Sharing stories of mishaps that brightened the day.

They whisper of rain, a peculiar thing,
How puddles became fountains, oh what joy they bring!
With tales of the sun, and its warm, golden rays,
Each leaf finds a voice, and a reason to play.

In the wild, there's adventure, with laughter to share,
For the leaves of the trees have stories to spare.
As seasons change colors, they bust out in cheer,
Leaves speaking in joy, for all those who hear.

The Melody of the Garden's Heart

In the garden at dawn, the flowers all hum,
While the bees start to bumble, with a comical drum.
Petals sway lightly, in a rhythm so sweet,
As the butterflies join, making dances on feet.

There's a rose with a knack for salsa so bold,
While the tulips all giggle, their stories unfold.
The daisies tap toes, on the soft, dewy grass,
And the sunflowers grin, when the bunnies all pass.

With glee they compete, each one a fine star,
Saying, "I can out-twist you, just watch me go far!"
But when shadows grow longer, they rest in delight,
As the moon joins the party, shining silver and bright.

In melodies sweet, the garden delights,
With laughter of life, and whimsical sights.
Each bloom holds a joke, and a tale to impart,
Together they sing, the song of the heart.

Enigma of the Wildflower Stories

Wildflowers bloom with quirks, what a sight,
With stories to tell from morning till night.
The daisies would brag about their bold stance,
While the violets whisper secrets to prance.

A dandelion's wish, quite misunderstood,
Once tried to be serious, but laughter's a good.
The breeze teased it gently, blew seeds all around,
And it chuckled aloud, at the joy that it found.

Clover in green, claimed to hold luck,
But tripped on a rock, with a silly pluck.
The wildflowers giggled, in colors so bright,
As they danced o'er the fields, from morning to night.

In the meadows there's wisdom wrapped up in jest,
Where the wildflowers weave tales that are simply the best.
Together they flourish, with laughs full of cheer,
Creating a tapestry, vivid and clear.

Odes to the Twisting Vines

The vines twist and turn, like dancers they play,
In a joyful ballet, they sway night and day.
With leaves as their partners, they twirl and they spin,
And whisper sweet secrets, as the fun begins.

A grapevine would boast of the best vintage wine,
But slipped on a twig, which was not too divine.
The ivy then chuckled, while watching the scene,
Saying, "Let's toast to bloopers, for life is a dream!"

The wisteria joined, with a puff and a sway,
Entangled with laughter, they brightened the day.
While tendrils looped round, with a giggly shout,
Claiming, "We're not lost, just having a route!"

In corners of gardens, their stories unfold,
With curls and with twists, they're both witty and bold.
As they dance through the breeze, in the sun's warm embrace,
Each vine shares its charm, with style and with grace.

Reflections of a Rooted Legacy

In a garden where the plants spill,
A stubborn weed thinks it's a thrill.
It claims a throne, a grand parade,
Yet all it does is spread and invade.

The elder sage with gnarled bark,
Whispers secrets after dark.
"Dig me up? You must be jesting!
My roots have quite a history resting!"

A sprout so small, it tries to dance,
Trips over leaves—a clumsy prance.
The daisies giggle, the roses cheer,
"Keep trying, buddy, we've got your rear!"

The tomato feels it's quite the chef,
Dreams of sauces that flaunt its heft.
But on the vine, it learns with dread,
It's just a sidekick to buttered bread.

Whispers Beneath the Canopy

Beneath the leaves, a secret bunch,
Squirrels plot their foodie lunch.
"That acorn's mine!" one claims brave,
But winds of fate make him a knave.

A mushroom giggles, wearing a crown,
"I'm the fairest of them in town!"
Yet clouds above begin to frown,
And drown him in their watery gown.

The ferns unite to share a jest,
"Who's got the biggest, greenest crest?"
They flaunt their fronds with feathery flair,
Ignoring all the weeds that dare.

An owl hoots, "I've seen it all!"
A passing breeze begins to brawl.
"Your roots are deep, but so is your face,
You missed my party; it's quite the disgrace!"

When the Petals Sing

In gardens gay, the flowers meet,
They start to hum a lively beat.
The roses swirl in twirling glee,
While tulips sway, so joyfully!

A daffodil proclaims, "I'm bold!"
As marigolds spin tales retold.
The lilies laugh, their voices bright,
"We're nature's stars—come share the light!"

A bumblebee joins, buzzing along,
He claims he's great, he's never wrong.
"I'll win a race! Just watch my speed,"
But stumbles back, a clumsy breed.

At dusk, the petals start to yawn,
And with the night, the fun is gone.
Yet dreams of blooms will still play on,
In whispered notes of a new dawn.

The Tapestry of Botanical Whimsy

In the garden, where the colors clash,
A gourd wears shades with quite a splash.
"I'm an artist!" it boasts with pride,
But it trips on vines that twist and slide.

The daisies dance, a frolicking crew,
Each takes a turn to show what's new.
One steps ahead, a royal blunder,
Falls face-first in the soil with thunder.

Herbs gossip softly, they love the chat,
"Basil says mint's a spoiled brat!"
Yet rosemary rolls its eyes in glee,
"At least I'm not stuck in soup, you'll see!"

Then comes a bug, a self-made star,
"I'm the fashion queen!" not near, but far.
Yet when she struts, she skips the cue,
And lands in a pot, her dreams askew.

In the Company of Thorns

In a garden full of cheer,
The thorns hold court, never fear.
They jest and dance, so very spry,
While petals blush and shy away.

Roses laugh, they roll their eyes,
Thorns pull pranks, to great surprise.
"We're sharp, but have a point to make!"
A chaotic waltz, for goodness' sake!

Bumblebees buzz, they can't complain,
As thorns enact their wild campaign.
With every poke, a laughter's grown,
In this garden, mischief's shown!

So, if you stroll where blossoms glow,
Beware the thorns that steal the show.
With humor stitched in every prick,
These jester stems make nature tick!

The Soliloquy of the Stem

A stem stood proud beneath the sun,
"My leaves are green, my jokes are fun!
I twist and twirl with elegant flair,
While watching bees pollinate with care."

"Oh, daisies giggle without a rhyme,
But I've got jokes that stand the test of time!
What did the vine say to the bud?
'Stop leafing around—you're just a dud!'"

Yet, a nearby twig gave a little sigh,
"Your humor, dear stem, is awfully spry.
But while you jest, don't forget your goals,
We're not just plants—we're nature's trolls!"

So, spinning tales with snickers sewn,
This witty stem enjoyed the throne.
A soliloquy of laughter and light,
In the garden's stage, a comical sight!

Nature's Poetic Expanse

In fields where wildflowers giggle,
Each petal's dance makes mewiggle.
A sunflower whispered, big and wise,
"Life's all about enjoying the rise!"

Trees gossip softly with rustling glee,
"Did you see that bug? It can't even see!"
They poke fun at the mushrooms' hats,
"Clumsy little fungi, flat as mats!"

Underneath the sky, a mirthful spree,
Every creature joins this frolic spree.
Nature's stage, where all is bright,
Creating giggles as day turns night.

So if you wander through this expanse,
Join in the laughter, take your chance.
With humor sprouting in every nook,
Be part of nature's joyful book!

Florals and Fragments

In the mix of blooms, odd ones thrive,
Petals blush, bees take a dive.
Dandelions yell, "We're here to stay!"
While tulips sway in a graceful play.

Orchids boast, "We're rare and fine!"
But fickle daisies roll in the vine.
"Look who's prancing, thinking they're grand,
But watch us scatter, like grains of sand!"

Each floral fragment has tales to share,
Stories laced in fragrant air.
"Yesterday's raindrop was quite the tease,
It dripped on me with such sweet ease!"

So laugh it off in the garden spree,
Where every bloom longs to be free.
In florals and fragments, joy takes flight,
Mixing nature's quirks with pure delight!

Flora's Echoes Throughout Time

In gardens where the daisies laugh,
The roses tell a cheeky tale,
Of bees who dance like silly staff,
And butterflies that never fail.

A dandelion's mock salute,
To passing clouds that roll and play,
While tulips wear a charming suit,
And giggle softly every day.

The violets gossip by the gate,
Of secrets shared beneath the moon,
While sturdy thistles speculate,
On who will reach the sun next June.

With every bloom a story spun,
Of whispers echoing through the years,
Nature's jest still just begun,
In laughter wrapped in foliage's cheers.

Sunlight's Company Among the Foliage

Sunlight tickles leaves up high,
As branches sway in playful glee,
The shadows dance as if to fly,
In this wild party, nature's spree.

A squirrel dons a cap of green,
With acorns bouncing in parade,
While lizards flaunt a glimmering sheen,
And frogs croak tunes that won't soon fade.

The flowers wink at passing bees,
Trading jokes of nectar bliss,
As breezes join with gentle tease,
This is the scene you wouldn't miss.

Their laughter swells like summer sun,
Beneath the canopy so bright,
In nature's play, the joy is spun,
Where daylight turns to sweet delight.

The Narrative of the Petal-Fingered Wind

The wind, it twirls with dainty grace,
And picks up petals on its way,
It jests and pokes 'round every place,
Leaving blooms in disarray.

A bloom in blue calls out for aid,
"Stop! You've tussled all my style!"
But giggles follow, lightly prayed,
From petals blown a dizzy mile.

As leaves join in, they'd cackle loud,
While gusts perform their merry waltz,
Beneath the sky, a laughing crowd,
Nature's whimsy has no faults.

And when at last it starts to fade,
The flowers sigh, "What a delight!"
In every twist, a jokester made,
As dusk prepares to steal the light.

Botanical Ballads of Yesteryears

Once lived a sunflower quite absurd,
Who fancied chat with every bee,
Its lofty tales would often blurt,
As bees around would nod with glee.

The marigolds chimed in with cheer,
Reciting tales from gardens past,
Of moonlit nights and laughter clear,
Where every bloom, a die was cast.

A creeping vine with tales of flair,
Spun yarns of troubles on the trail,
While squirrels gathered round to share,
In oak trees' arms, a merry tale.

Together they conjure joyous light,
With every petal, every grin,
These ballads bloom in pure delight,
As nature hums, the fun begins.

Tales of the Forest's Grasp

In a tree with a grin, a squirrel took a seat,
He shared tales of acorns, a nutty treat.
A raccoon joined in, with a mask on his face,
Claiming all nuts should be kept in a case.

A fox made it clear, he was king of the wood,
But tripped on a branch, oh, isn't he good?
The laughter erupted, the leaves danced in cheer,
As the forest kept sharing its tales loud and clear.

With owls hooting loudly, and fireflies bright,
They all had a party, it lasted till night.
The twigs held their drinks, and acorns with flair,
A gathering of fun, without a single care.

So if you're once lost in a forest so grand,
Listen closely to whispers of creatures so planned.
With tales in the air and giggles that last,
You'll find every tree holds a story so vast.

Dance of the Fragrant Petals

In a garden of blooms, a bee took to dance,
He twirled with a rose, hoping for a chance.
But the daisy was dizzy, she spun too fast,
'It's pollen, not tango!' she shouted with blast.

A posy of lilies had tea by the gate,
'We sip with the bees, or we risk a sad fate.'
They laughed and they whispered, oh what a sight,
But the butterflies giggled, and took off in flight.

The tulips were bold, with a waltz in their sway,
While the lilacs just snickered at their clumsy display.
'You'll trip on a petal!' they hollered in glee,
But the blooms just kept dancing, wild as can be.

So next time you wander through flowers in bloom,
Watch for the dancers, they'll brighten your gloom.
With laughter and fragrance, they spin and they twirl,
A garden of joy, in a colorful whirl.

Among the Twining Vines

In a tangle of vines that twist and entwine,
A worm threw a party, said, 'Come sip some wine!'
The snails brought the glasses, so shiny and round,
But they wobbled and trembled, fell right to the ground.

The ivy rolled in, sporting a new hat,
'This trend is for vines, just look where I'm at!'
But the thorns did complain, 'That's terribly bold,
I'd prick you with envy, or so I've been told.'

A butterfly fluttered, with sweet tiny treats,
While the grasses just giggled, shared snacks called 'seeds.'
They cheered with delight, as the fireflies gave light,
While the moss made a stage for an impromptu night.

So when you find green, with laughter and fun,
Know that the vines have already begun.
With stories and snacks growing wild in the field,
The best of the parties is nature revealed.

Epistles of the Silent Blooms

In a quiet old garden where whispers reside,
The flowers began writing, their secrets inside.
'We bloomed here in spring, but oh what a plot,
The tulips teased peonies, and daisies got hot.'

The lilies exchanged notes, with tales of the rain,
While the pansies pondered on the joys of the pain.
'What's that over there? A bug in a suit?'
They giggled, they shuffled, oh how they looked cute!

Hummingbirds hovered, collecting the tales,
Of mishaps and blossoms with vibrant sails.
It's not just the petals they shared in the night,
But laughter and wit in the soft moonlight.

So should you behold all the blooms' funny lore,
Know every petal has a tale at its core.
In the silence of gardens, the stories will bloom,
With giggles and whispers that light up the gloom.

The Saga of Twining Vines

In a garden where creepers climb,
A vine told jokes, oh so sublime.
It laughed at the fence, gave it a poke,
'You can't hold me back, I'm a punny bloke!'

The roses shook, with petals aglow,
'Oh dear vine, your wit is quite the show!'
They swayed in the breeze, chuckling with glee,
While the daisies joined in with a giggly spree.

One day the vine thought it would try,
To wrap itself round a passing fly.
'You're stuck now, bug, in my leafy embrace!'
But the fly just buzzed and flew off like a race!

Now after that day, the vine knows well,
A garden's true joke is a story to tell.
So it twists and it twirls, full of its fun,
Crafting tales in the sun, under the laughing run.

Mosaic of Leaves and Dreams

In a patch of shade where dreams mix and play,
A leaf made a wish on a bright sunny day.
It wished for a dance and a chance to be seen,
To show off its colors, so bold and so green.

The winds heard the leaf and gave it a spin,
It twirled with the light, oh what a great grin!
The daisies nearby played a tune from the fray,
While the leaf whirled in circles, like no other ballet.

Then came a squirrel, with a sack full of nuts,
He joined in the dance, a mischief, but what?!
The leaf laughed so hard, of course he'd be late,
As he tripped on a twig, oh, the laughter was great!

With each little gust, a new story would thrive,
In the mosaic of leaves, where all dreams come alive.
They danced with the sun, as the shadows all played,
Creating a laughter that never would fade.

Essence of the Green Tapestry

In a tapestry woven with emerald threads,
Lived a critter named Spike with bright, plump dreads.
He swore he'd out-sneak a sly garden cat,
But cartwheeled right into a pile of compost flat!

With petals a-flutter, the daisies asked why,
'Is it fashion or folly that's caught you, oh my?'
Spike laughed with a chuckle, 'It's style, pure and true!'
'Just getting my greens on; what say you?'

But the cat crept closer, a whiskered delight,
'You do have a flair, but I prefer my bite!'
Spike leapt from the compost, with laughter and glee,
'I bet you can't catch me, under this tree!'

So went the laughter, in the gardens so bright,
Where Spike would dodge sharply, a comical sight.
With giggles and grins, they danced around fuss,
In the essence of nature, all fill with great trust.

Fables from the Floral Realm

In a realm of blossoms, where stories do bloom,
A tulip told fables, dispelling the gloom.
She spun tales of bees, who served up their thrills,
With nectar so sweet, giving joy to the chills.

'Look at that rose,' she winked with a smile,
'With thorns on her stem, she can be quite vile!'
The daisies exploded in laughter and fun,
As petals would dance, under bright morning sun.

'But let's not forget our friend, dandy lion!'
A dandelion puff, with seeds in a mine.
'He floats on the wind, with a bubbly great cheer,
Spreading wisdom and joy, as he gallops near!'

With petals all curious, they gathered around,
To hear every tale from the floral ground.
In the laughter of blossoms, the wisdom unfurled,
In a lively, funny, and fabulous world!

Fables of the Flourishing Realm

In a garden where the daisies dance,
A potato once considered romance.
It dressed in petals, bright and spry,
But the bees just buzzed and passed it by.

A cucumber thought it wise to flirt,
With a flower in a flouncy shirt.
"I'm not your type," the tulip said,
"I like my dates all leaf and bread."

The carrots laughed beneath their crowns,
At a radish wearing silly gowns.
"You're too bold for this garden place,
You might just be a veggie disgrace!"

The sunflowers chuckled at the plot,
Watching veggies give it all they got.
In this realm of greens and glee,
Laughter blooms like lemon tea.

The Soliloquy of the Unruly Garden

In a patch where chaos seems to reign,
A rogue weed claims its steady gain.
"I'm the king of tangled lines!"
With braids of roots and stubborn vines.

The carrots quip, "You need a brush!"
"Your hair's a mess, it's quite the crush!"
But Mr. Weed with a wink replied,
"Beauty's in the mess, come join my ride!"

The cabbage rolls its leafy eyes,
"You're a jester in disguise!"
But the flower blurted out with glee,
"At least you're not a bag of peas!"

So under sun and whirling breeze,
The garden chuckled with such ease.
In wild winds they do concede,
Laughter's seed is all we need.

Confessions of the Thorned Sentinel

Among the blooms, the thorned one sighed,
"I guard the garden, but I feel fried!"
With sharp wit and a sharper spine,
He told the rose, "You're quite divine!"

The rose just laughed, "Oh, dear friend,
Your prickly ways have no end!"
"I watch for pests, I stand my ground,
Yet all I get is trouble found!"

The daisies danced; they gently swayed,
Pretending not to hear the fray.
"Oh Sentinel, you need some tea,
With sugar sweet, and more carefree!"

Yet every thorn has a tale to share,
Of bees that land without a care.
In the garden's heart, all agree,
Even thorns can find some glee!

The Harmonies of Curled Foliage

Oh hear the leaves, they sing a tune,
Under the light of a cheeky moon.
Their spirals whirl in joyous flight,
Making the garden feel just right.

A fussy fern fluffed up with pride,
Announced to all, "I'm nature's guide!"
But a clover with a spunky flair,
Cried, "We're all fabulous in this lair!"

Laughter echoed through the trees,
As the wildflowers swayed with ease.
"When it rains, we take our chance,
To twirl in puddles and laugh and dance!"

With every twist and vibrant hue,
The foliage sang its merry tune.
In this garden, fun blooms wide,
Where every leaf's along for the ride!

Petal-Laden Reveries

Once a flower dreamed to sprout so high,
But it tripped on a bee, oh my, oh my!
With petals in disarray, it did a dance,
Laughing hard at fate's peculiar chance.

A cactus tried to join a flower show,
But forgot its outfit—prickly and slow.
The judge just rolled his eyes, gave a grin,
"You're not quite ready, but oh, come on in!"

In the garden, a daffodil glowed with pride,
But a squirrel stole its hat, it couldn't hide.
"I shall wear my leaves!" it declared with flair,
As the furry thief chuckled, without a care.

A rose once told a joke, but alas, it failed,
The petals giggled, but the humor was veiled.
"Why do we wilt?" it queried in jest,
"Because laughter makes us bloom, at best!"

Whispers of the Wild

In the woods, a tree tried to sing a tune,
But it rustled its leaves, like a woeful loon.
"Please hold your applause," it swayed with grace,
While the critters all laughed at its leafy face.

A raccoon once planned to bake a pie,
But mistook dirt for flour, oh my, oh my!
The forest held a feast, under stars so bright,
'Dessert's a bit gritty, but such a delight!''

A mushroom in purple wore quite a crown,
Declared itself queen of the forest town.
"Bow down, little bugs!" it shouted with glee,
But they rolled on the ground, too busy to see.

And then came a rabbit, with carrots galore,
It tripped on a root, then fell to the floor.
"I'm a dancing veggie!" it loudly proclaimed,
While the forest erupted, all giggles unchained.

A hedgehog, so proud, tried to play a flute,
But ended up sounding like a clumsy brute.
Still, all the woodland creatures joined the hype,
For their band of the wild made the evening ripe!

The Art of Botanical Tales

There once was a seed, quite eager to grow,
But it ended up sprouting all in a row.
The flowers had formed, a delightful brigade,
But the weeds interjected, with silly charades.

A tulip told stories of sunny delights,
As daisies just nodded through all of its flights.
"We bloom in the spring!" they cheered with a twist,
While a sunflower winked, "I need a huge list!"

A petunia, feeling quite sly and aloof,
Decided to recite with a sassy, aloof.
"I'm the best flower!" it boasted with pride,
But tripped on a root, and the garden just cried.

In the greenhouse, a fern just grew quite a lot,
And claimed it was wise, not just a big pot.
"Listen to me!" it affirmed with some glee,
But a beetle just buzzed, "You're all leaves, can't you see?"

Yet amidst all the laughter, a daisies parade,
Sing songs of the garden, their friendship unwavering made.
The art of their tales danced on petals so fair,
For life in the blooms is joy we can share!

Threads of the Growing Season

In spring's early morning, a blossom took stage,
With enthusiasm high, it cleared the front page.
"Watch me grow big!" it exclaimed with delight,
Then stumbled on dew, in the soft morning light.

A garden of veggies hosted a race,
But the lettuce felt dizzy, just lost in the chase.
The carrots sprinted forth, with flair and with style,
As tomatoes rolled in, but past them, a mile!

A pumpkin once boasted, "I'm the king of the lot!"
But slipped on some dirt, and oh was it caught!
With a vine tied in knots, it still grinned at the crowd,
"Well folks, that's what happens when you're too proud!"

A flower pot pondered what it would be,
"I'd love to be famous, just wait and see!"
But then it just leaked and made quite a mess,
With soil on its leaves—such a royal distress!

As summer arrived, the garden was bright,
With laughter and chatter, it felt just so right.
Each thread of the season, a tale to repeat,
In gardens of joy, life dances on feet!

Nectar and Nostalgia

Bees tap-dance on blooms so bright,
Wrestling with petals in morning light.
Hummingbirds hover, sipping sweet dreams,
While my cat plots mischief, or so it seems.

Old trees gossip in rustling leaves,
Telling tales of the tricks up their sleeves.
I swear one winked when I took a peep,
Probably dreaming of secrets to keep.

Frogs wear crowns in muddy thrones,
Croaking out tunes, full of silly tones.
The pond's a party, with laughter, no doubt,
While turtles giggle as they try to sneak out.

Upon a dais of daisies bright,
A snail recites poetry every night.
But when I applaud, he just hides away,
Maybe stage fright? Who's to say?

Shadows of the Foliage

Underneath the leafy glow,
Squirrels chase shadows, putting on a show.
With acorns flying, oh what a sight,
They plan their next heist by the moonlight!

The winds whisper secrets, tickle the grass,
While crickets practice their nightly jazz.
The fireflies twinkle, oh what a dance,
As the owl looks down, caught in a trance.

Mice wear tiny hats, so full of flair,
Planning a gala, with cheese to share.
But the cat's in the corner, peeking around,
Dreaming of dinner, with hope he's not found.

Oh, the laughter that fills the night air,
As shadows play games without a care.
Nature's a circus when daytime is done,
With each furry friend just ready for fun!

The Dance of the Greenery

Ferns twirl gracefully in a breeze,
While daisies shake heads, all with ease.
I watched a butterfly do the cha-cha,
As ants formed a conga line, hurrah!

Mushrooms canoodle in a whimsical way,
Making friends with grass blades, come what may.
The flowers, they giggle, bloom after bloom,
While the wind teases, leading them to zoom.

A ladybug leads, with spots like confetti,
As the garden erupts into a dance pretty.
The tomatoes roll in, they want a turn,
Rooting for veggies, oh how they yearn!

Twilight descends, and the dancers are tired,
With crickets playing lullabies inspired.
Nature applauds, it's the end of the show,
As the stars wink down, this magical glow.

Snapshots of Nature's Canvas

A snapshot taken with a butterfly grin,
While the daisies proudly wear their pin.
A rainbow of colors, vibrant and bright,
Every petal a story, what a delight!

The river shares laughs in rippling tones,
Echoing secrets to the pebbled stones.
Fish flash their smiles, while frogs do their part,
Oh, the snapshots taken, straight from the heart!

Clouds fluff up like cotton candy dreams,
Hitching rides on sunlight, or so it seems.
Birds pose for portraits on branches so high,
While squirrels photobomb, oh me, oh my!

Even the moon takes a selfie or two,
With cheeky stars winking, as if they knew.
Through the lens of laughter, nature unfolds,
In snapshots of fun, her stories told.

Regalia of the Garden Spirits

In the garden, spirits prance,
Wearing leaves, they twist and dance.
One lost his shoe, oh what a sight!
A dandelion blooms in pure delight.

Butterflies gossip on a sunlit beam,
They spill the tea on a sneaky dream.
A snail with shades thinks he's so cool,
While worms sneak rumors—who's the fool?

Gnomes in hats a bit too grand,
They tip their caps to the flowers' stand.
A ruckus bursts from the hedgehog's grieve,
When nettles dance and yell, "We leave!"

Oh, the whiskers on the cats do sway,
As they plot mischief through the day.
What laughter caught in the rustling leaves,
In this garden where nothing deceives!

Echoes of Botanical Legends

In shadows deep where legends loom,
A cactus tells tales of endless bloom.
With prickly humor, he jests aloud,
While violets giggle, forming a crowd.

The willow warns of a cheeky breeze,
That steals the hats from dainty trees.
"Protect your blooms!" the petals shout,
As dandelions roll, there's no doubt.

A mushroom cap dons a crown so bright,
Spinning yarns of a fairy's flight.
But with each twist, they trip and fall,
Creating a ruckus, a joyous brawl!

Time flows slow where whimsy grows,
And laughter from petals freely flows.
Every twig holds a secret spree,
In this realm of giggles, wild and free!

The Heartbeat of the Undergrowth

Beneath the leaves, the crunching sound,
Is critters dancing all around.
A spider weaves with shades of flair,
While beetles argue, unaware.

A tunnel's home, a mole does dig,
Avoiding tosses from a sneaky twig.
The ants march on, a troop in line,
Trading snacks, oh how divine!

The fungi chuckle in quiet mirth,
Plotting adventures beneath the earth.
A gopher's story is hard to believe,
As he sips tea from a leaf he weaves.

In this chaos, heartbeats blend,
As nature laughs, on friends depend.
A symphony of giggles in shades so bright,
In the undergrowth's playful light!

Poetry in Nature's Weeds

In the muddy patch, weeds take stage,
With a tap dance, they engage.
A thistle prances with a prickle show,
While lilies snicker, "Oh no, oh no!"

The dandelions puff, whispering jokes,
Making fun of the turning folks.
"Watch our petals scatter wide,
As we giggle and spin with pride!"

A patch of clover lifts its head,
Sharing tales of the other plants' dread.
A rogue chicken pecks, a fool with glee,
While the grasshoppers bounce, carefree!

Amidst the laughter, blooms converge,
In this world where antics surge.
From the messy weedy, life will sprout,
Full of laughter—without a doubt!

The Legacy of the Laceleaf

In a garden so bright, where the greens like to dance,
A laceleaf once claimed, 'I've got moves with a chance.'
But when pruned too short, oh, what a sad tale,
It spun round and shouted, 'I'm doomed to be frail!'

With each passing day, it grew tall and so proud,
Throwing shade at the daisies, it laughed quite loud.
The squirrels would stare, baffled by its pose,
As the laceleaf made jokes about all of the oaks.

The rainy days came, and a thundercloud loomed,
'Not me!' it declared, 'I'll never be doomed!'
Splashing through puddles, it twirled in the rain,
Leaving all of its friends just a bit of disdain.

Yet in spring when it bloomed, the laughter returned,
Every leaf showed a grin, every green stem discerned.
With stories of mischief and tales of pure glee,
The laceleaf became legend, it thrived wild and free.

An Epic of Evergreen Trysts

In a forest so lush, where the pine trees convene,
Two evergreens plotted a love so serene.
Whispers of romance exchanged in the breeze,
They giggled and blushed, swaying gently with ease.

One pine said with flair, 'I've got needles for days!'
The fir rolled its eyes, 'But my scent truly slays.'
They didn't mind fighting, it's all just a game,
As they twirled 'round the trunk, setting hearts all aflame.

But the moody oak frowned, watching them play,
'Why pine when you can be friends with my sway?'
They laughed and replied, 'You're too stiff, can't you see?

We'd rather be tangled in wild jubilee!'

So season by season, their friendship took flight,
With laughter aplenty, through day and through night.
Together they danced, in the dew's soft embrace,
An epic of love in this green, glorious place.

Whispers of the Botanical Muse

In a pot on the shelf, with a view of the sun,
A plant said aloud, 'Life's just begun!'
It practiced its lines in the mirror each morn,
Dreaming of stages where laughter was born.

'Oh leafy companion, I've got quite a dream,
To make all the flowers giggle, it seems!'
But the cactus just snorted, with spikes of disdain,
'Staying rooted is wise, young bud, don't be vain.'

Yet undeterred, the sprout took a chance,
It danced in its pot, the whole summer at a glance.
The daisies cheered loud, while the tulips just swayed,
The muse of the garden, with charm it allayed.

As the sun started setting, they all joined the show,
Each petal and leaf, with a unique kind of glow.
A botanical revel, where joy came to fuse,
With whispers of laughter, the world it enthused.

Leaves of Memory

In autumn's embrace, when the leaves turned to gold,
A maple told stories, far better than old.
With each rustling whisper, it spoke of the past,
Of acorns so tiny and saplings so vast.

'Oh, remember the days when we danced in the breeze?
We played hide and seek, oh, such merriment, please!'
The oak shared a chuckle, recalling the fun,
'Like the time that the winds thought we'd all come undone.'

'Let's meet at the creek, where the willows will sway,
For laughter is best when shared in the play.'
The pines stood in awe, as the stories unfurled,
Each leaf had a giggle, a tale to be twirled.

So as winter approached, with a blanket of white,
They vowed to keep laughing, even through the night.
For memories linger, like greenery spry,
With leaves full of laughter that never say goodbye.

The Silenced Bloom's Tale

In a garden so bright, one flower stood tall,
Only to sneeze when bugs came to call.
"Excuse me!" it blurted, quite full of shame,
Its petals all fluttered, yet none knew its name.

The bees held their laughter, the ants joined in too,
"It's just a missed joke!" said the morning dew.
The flower turned red, like the sun at noon,
And vowed to tell puns on the next afternoon.

It practiced all night, with a wee little gnome,
Who chuckled and chortled, then felt right at home.
When finally dawned, the whole garden roared,
For the jokes made from petals, were wildly adored!

Now that bloom is a star, hosting guests far and wide,
With jokes that would make the shyest bugs glide.
It learned that laughter is truly the key,
In a garden full of oddities, we're all funny, you see!

Chronicles of Shaded Peace

Under the trees, where the sunlight feels shy,
Lived a squirrel named Nutters, who loved to fly high.
With a banana for wings, he'd leap and he'd soar,
But crashed in a puddle—oh, what a loud roar!

A wise old tortoise, in slow-moving grace,
Watched Nutters take flight, with a grin on his face.
"Your antics are joyful, but that jump was too bold!"
Nutters shook water off, with fur oh so cold.

"Next time I'm flying, I'll bring a snack treat!"
He clambered up branches, with such nimble feet.
But instead of his courage, he grabbed acorn stew,
And fell in the bushes, to dreams that he flew.

The trees rustled softly, as laughter took root,
For Nutters the brave, he's quite an astute!
With friends all around, they healed his pride,
In the shade of the park, where silliness won't hide.

Ciphers of Nature's Hand

A rock and a twig held a secret so clear,
That friendship blooms loud, when you lend a kind ear.
The twig liked to gossip, the rock was quite stout,
Yet their stories were funny, with laughter about.

One day as they chatted, a breeze passed on through,
With leaves dancing gladly, and the sky shining blue.
"What's the best joke?" inquired the old stone,
"It's when you trip over roots, then claim you've outgrown!"

The twig nearly tumbled, as it shook with mirth,
While the rock just rolled on, a giggle of worth.
And so they exchanged, their best tales from the earth,
Reminding all creatures of joy's endless birth.

In the quiet of woods, where the whispers now cling,
A rock and a twig make the laughter take wing.
They cipher their magic, through each chuckle and sigh,
Crafting tales of joy, as the clouds drift on by.

The Timeless Dance of Roots

In a patch of deep soil, where secrets do hide,
Roots tangled in laughter, as they wiggled with pride.
"I tickled your neighbor!" one root did proclaim,
As the earth shook with giggles, delighted by the game.

"Oh, do it again!" shouted one leaf from above,
For roots have their parties, spreading chuckles and love.
They danced and they jiggled, beneath the great trees,
With a wink to the tulips that swayed in the breeze.

But one root grew jealous, with an itch to take flight,
"I'll spin wildly, watch me! It will be such a sight!"
It twirled with such fervor, that the soil did shake,
And neighbors all chuckled as that root made a break!

Down in the depths, where the fun never ends,
Dance on, little roots, with your whimsical bends.
For life underground is a carnival, bright,
Where laughter erupts, even hiding from light.

Myths of the Verdant Haven

In a garden lush, a snail wore shoes,
Trotting around to share its views.
It claimed to be fast, in a rush to explain,
But folks just laughed—what a funny campaign!

The daisies debated the best dance style,
While the cacti critiqued with an adorable smile.
In this world of green, where stories unfold,
Every plant has a tale, eager to be told.

Frogs throw parties, they leap with delight,
Inviting all critters for a wild night.
With tunes from the crickets, the evening's a blast,
Their revelry echoes, a memory to last.

A wise old oak saw the comical plight,
Of a turkey that tried to take off in flight.
"Stay grounded," it chuckled, "you're better on land,
Leave the soaring to birds—it's part of the plan!"

The Garden's Hidden Narratives

There's a gopher who dreams of being a star,
He practices lines while munching on a carrot bar.
His friends roll their eyes, but he winks with flair,
In his mind, he's famous, with fans everywhere.

A cucumber once thought it could be a tree,
It stretched and it strained, had a grand fantasy.
But with laughter, the radishes shouted with glee,
"Just stay in the patch, and we'll all watch your spree!"

Butterflies gossip from petal to leaf,
Whispers of romance, or stories of grief.
But when a breeze rustles, they scatter and flee,
"Oh no, not the gossip! We'll fly out to sea!"

Squirrels debate who can jump the most high,
While a lazy old tortoise rolls by with a sigh.
"Jumping is fine, but slow wins the race,"
He chuckles and shuffles, a smile on his face.

Penchant for the Verdure

In a patch where the weeds think they rule the land,
A dandelion said, "I'll make a grand stand!"
But each little puff that went sailing away,
Brought laughter of bees at the close of the day.

A radish parade rolled with much pomp and flair,
Waving their greens and dropping soil everywhere.
"Look at us go!" cried a cheeky new sprout,
As bugs pinched their sides and giggled about.

The sunflower on guard, keeping watch from above,
Spied a pair of worms who were tangled in love.
"Get a room!" they called, with a wink and a smile,
"Oh, the drama of roots—it's been fun for a while!"

When the rain comes down, with a plop and a splat,
The flowers just dance, "Oh, we do love that!"
And beetles on leaves make a quick little tune,
In this garden of joy, we all sing in June.

From Seeds to Serpentine Stories

In a plot full of seeds waiting to sprout,
A pumpkin was plotting a great twist to tout.
"I'll grow into a carriage, you'll see when I'm ripe,"
But all that he got was some old trash and hype.

An ivy creept up to the highest tall fence,
To match wits with a rabbit, oh, what a suspense!
"Let's see who can climb higher, come give it a shot,"
But the rabbit just laughed, "Your tales are a lot!"

Beneath the broad leaves, the soil held tight,
A troupe of ants staged a comedic fight.
With tiny little swords made of crumbs and of dirt,
They battled with gusto—what a funny spurt!

The sunflowers crowned themselves queen of the lane,
Boasting of visions while swaying with grain.
"Your dreams are just petals," the daisies would shout,
But the laughter that followed was what it's about!

Nature's Subtle Narratives

In gardens lush, a tale unfolds,
Where flowers gossip, secrets told.
The bees debate the best sweet treat,
While crickets dance on nimble feet.

A squirrel sneaks a daring bite,
The gardener shouts, "Hey! That's not right!"
But with a wink, the squirrel grins,
And scampers off with stolen wins.

The sun looks down, a bright old chap,
And giggles as the flowers nap.
A breeze brings laughter, quite a jest,
Nature's humor, truly best!

So listen close to leafy lore,
In every rustle, there's much more.
For laughter blooms where few have seen,
In verdant tales, both bold and green.

Portraits of the Elaborate Leaf

A leaf once wore a fancy coat,
It claimed a crown, sat like a goat.
With colors bright, it made quite a fuss,
Impressing all, even the bus.

A neighbor leaf was quite the brat,
With holes and spots, it looked like that!
Yet they played cards, a leafy crew,
In poker games, they always drew.

One day a gust made all go twirl,
The fancy leaf let out a whirl!
"Oh dear, my dress!" it cried in vain,
As the spotted one laughed, bright and plain.

Together they twinkled in the sun,
Two odd pals, who had such fun.
In nature's ball, they spun with glee,
In their leafy lives, both wild and free.

The Aria of the Thorny Bloom

A rose with thorns, oh quite the plight,
Declared a concert, to take flight.
With petals soft, it sang with glee,
While thorns just poked, "Don't hug me!"

The daisies laughed, a joyful crowd,
They knew the rose was far too proud.
Yet joined the show with petals bright,
A comedic twist in nature's light.

The chorus burst, a floral cheer,
With bees and bugs all gathering near.
Yet one wrong note made thorns prowl,
And all the blooms began to howl!

So sing they did, a hilarious fate,
Through prickling pokes, they learned to mate.
In thorny blooms, life found a way,
To laugh aloud at the end of day.

Stories in the Shade

Beneath the branches, shadows play,
Where whispered tales come out to stay.
A lizard chats with passing ants,
While sloths bring snacks and share their slants.

The old oak tells of storms it's braved,
While laughing winds feel quite enslaved.
A squirrel nods, quite wise and old,
"Your bark has stories yet untold!"

Beneath the leaves where sunbeams dare,
A dance of whispers fills the air.
The grass joins in, a secret club,
While flowers giggle in a hub.

So join the shade and lend an ear,
To nature's tales both bright and clear.
For in the quiet, we can find,
The funny side of life, so kind.

Stories Woven in Green

In the garden's corner, a tale unfolds,
A mischievous lizard, of antics bold.
He danced with the daisies, laughed with the bees,
Planting seeds of giggles among the trees.

The tulips were blushing, adorned in bright hue,
While jokes from the ferns flew, merry and true.
A snail caught a ride on a butterfly's back,
Sipping nectar dreams on the whimsical track.

Giggling leaves whispered secrets of fun,
Under the sunbeam, their laughter spun.
Nature's comedians, vibrant and spry,
Inviting us all to join in the jive.

From gnarled old roots to the fresh green tips,
Each blossom a punchline, no one can eclipse.
As the daylight fades into twilight's embrace,
A festival of chuckles lights up the space.

The Requiem of the Withering Leaf

Once a leaf, proud and lush, sat high on a bough,
It found itself in a storm, oh boy, what a row!
'Twas torn from its branch with a comic flail,
It spiraled and twirled, a leaf on a gale.

As it plummeted down in a dizzying flight,
It laughed with the branches, 'Just hold on tight!'
But alas, on the ground, it met a rough fate,
A squirrel chastised it, 'You're way too late!'

Jokers of nature all laughed at the scene,
A spectacle staged for a leaf's final glean.
Yet even in shadows, it twinkled with glee,
Finding joy in departing, as wild as can be.

So here's to that leaf, in its grand exit spree,
A reminder to jest, even when we're not free.
Each flutter, each tumble is surely a jest,
In the realm of the garden, we are all but a guest.

Sagas from the Thicket's Edge

At the thicket's edge, stories come alive,
Where critters are sages and pranks thrive.
A rabbit once said, 'Life's a grand joke!'
While a woodpecker pondered, tapping oak.

The bushes were shaking with laughter and cheer,
As ants claimed the prize for the funniest seer.
With ticklish roots and giggling vines,
Every twist in the path, a humorous sign.

Owl in his wisdom, with glasses in place,
Claimed to be serious, yet sported a face
That cracked into laughter, so sly and so wise,
A chuckle escaped through feathery sighs.

So join in the revels where tales intertwine,
At the thicket's edge, you'll be just fine.
The ruckus of nature is laughter's refrain,
In the heart of the woods, we're all slightly insane!

The Lament of the Wisteria

The wisteria blooms with a sway and a sigh,
Recalling the wits of her youth as they fly.
'With petals so purple, I was quite the delight,
But now as I droop, I don't feel so bright.'

Mockingbirds chirp as they gather in jest,
'Oh, wisteria dear, you were truly the best!
Your vines were a party, a twist of pure fun,
Now look at you, darling, where has it run?'

An old bumblebee buzzed, with wisdom so keen,
'You've danced in the moonlight, don't dwell on the screen!
Embrace all the moments, the laughter and play,
Each wrinkle tells tales of a vibrant bouquet.'

So the wisteria laughed, her spirit aglow,
Finding joy in her plight, a soft purple show.
In the garden of giggles, she claimed her own space,
A legend who bloomed with hilarious grace.

www.ingramcontent.com/pod-product-compliance
Lightning Source LLC
Chambersburg PA
CBHW071830160426
43209CB00003B/267